When My Soul Speaks, I Scribe...*Poetry*

Bettina "Gold" Wilkerson

In loving memory of
Vanessa I. E. Cooper

*You are a poem in my heart written with an
indelible ink, never to be washed away…*

DEDICATION

If I state I created this body of work alone, I would not be completely truthful. I believe who we are (or who we claim to be) is a reflection of our experiences, and our connections. Given this perspective, it seems only right for my spirit to dedicate this book t o my ancestors, may they continue to rest in peace and may their spirits continue to guide me, my parents who nurtured me and provided a safe place for me to grow and explore my ambitions, my aunts and uncles who have loved me unconditionally since my first breath, my sister and brother whose love and friendship I could never be without, my cousins with whom I share an unbreakable bond, my teachers and mentors who taught me how to be a leader, my friends who have been with me through the darkest of times and shared the brightest of moments, my incredible girls Rashauna and Alexandria (you make me better), and to the random stranger whose eyes, hand or touch I may connect with along the way—I dedicate this book to all of you. For it is the moments you have shared with me that have become my voice to scribe; and for this, I am forever grateful.

CONTENTS

No Place Like Home

The Awakening

Truth & Pain

Love Is So Many Things

For Those
Who Blazed the Path
For Me to Walk Upon

Where Do We Go From Here?

No Place Like HOME

PO'KEEPSIE, MY KEEPSIE

U-PUKU-IPI-SING!

The reed covered lodge
by the little water place
Native American
PO'Keepsie
MY Keepsie

Not quite the urban jungle I grew up in
but you have sidewalks
        and I like that.

I was not born/bred here
did not go to your schools here
rip roar through your streets here
or play in your yards here

my experience in Poughkeepsie
may be different from yours here

It's having
a perfectly scrambled egg
at Alex's Diner

That's important to me
I enjoy my food here

It's like being a caterpillar
morphing into a butterfly
and realizing you have wings
to fly
        fly
                fly here

It's lying on the banks of the Hudson
looking up at the Walkway
wishing I was a local artist
like Michael White or Arnold Levine
so that I could paint the landscape
and the people walking above me here

It's being told as a child
that a tree grows in Brooklyn
only to discover
that a tree grows in Poughkeepsie
at the Family Partnership here

My experience in Poughkeepsie
is like going back in time
and sitting in a history class
the only difference is
I'm older now
          so I pay attention here.

It's discovering we were once
the capital of New York State
and the eleventh state
to ratify the Constitution here

It's knowing that
the Astors and the Vanderbilts
once had palatial homes
probably kicked back
on a hot summer's day and enjoyed
Matthew Vassar's brew here

Bettina "Gold" Wilkerson

My experience in Poughkeepsie
celebrates in the knowledge
that Jane Bolin
the first black female judge
was born here
the first Black female
to graduate Yale Law School
was born here

My experience is music here
it's rock n roll, folk and jazz
the Chance the Bardavon
and the Ciboney
it's where hip hop meets rock
from TiTo Montana
to the Anthony K Band
and spoken word blossoms
from the rhythm of the flow here

It's where art
can find a home
at the Barret Clay Works
the Cunneen Hackett Art Center
and the Mill Street Loft
where one finds the artist is to the canvas
the way water
              is to rain here.

My experience in Poughkeepsie
rejoices in knowing
the most powerful anti-slavery sermon
was preached on the eve
of Lincoln's inauguration
at the First Congregational Church here

And that Bill Duke
became a predator in pursuit of his career
and Elisa Donovan
wasn't clueless at all
as she set out to live her dream
and who would have known
in *An Affair To Remember*
that Richard Dennings was born here

My experience in Poughkeepsie
is part of a new history
not one which is antiquated or relegated
but one which is newly created and celebrated
by the merchants and the vendors
the painters and the sculptors
the singers and the dancers
and by the poets
and the people
      the people
            the people here!

U-PUKU-IPI-SING!

the reed covered lodge
by the little water place

Not quite the concrete jungle I grew up in
but you have sidewalks
        and I like that.

I was not born/bred here
did not go to your schools here
rip roar through your streets here
or play in your yards here

Bettina "Gold" Wilkerson

My experience in Po'Keepsie
may be different from yours here.

So when I hear someone say
"PO' Keepsie"
I say
"It's MY Keepsie
and We
            Are
                  Rich!"

WHERE I GREW uP

I grew up with the *clack clack!* of dominoes
landing on make shift table tops
        that sat upon milk crates
Bodegas filled with the sweet smell
of white cheese and salchichon

as a child I called it cha-chi-chon
who knew
a fifty cents piece please

The corner icy man
shouting "piragua piragua"
Yeshiva University and yarmulkes

This was my neighborhood and I loved it.

I loved it just because I belonged
to something greater than myself.
I was living amongst historical giants
like George Washington and Malcolm X
whose lives were resurrected
from the concrete beneath my feet
Bridges and buildings were built
to honor their names

So when I stood next to the four tall buildings
that seemed to touch the sky
I imagined I could leap them in a single bound
because my mind was never bound.

They would be the bridge
to connect me to the rainbow

and I would grow up
and tell stories of these days.

There were no white picket fences
but there were plenty of dreams
My friends were like Fat Albert's
        and Bebe's Kids, Little Rascals,
                Charlie Brown and Peanuts
                all rolled up into one,
But we were called "The Bridge Kids"

We were being flavored by salsa, merengue,
Afro-centric Cubano groove, good soul music,
Cadillacs, gangsta leans and all that—

The Heights!
This is where I grew up.

In my hood
most folks gave a damn
about someone else's child
because they gave a damn
about their own child

The word 'village'
was more than a seven letter word
or a catch phrase
and poor meant that you were born rich
with a sense of ethics

We were strong back then—built with courage
Because fists fights never
        turned into gun fights
                that turned into pact fights
viewed on You Tube Saturday nights—

We were never somebody else's fool.
And our assets
were not
where our
ass sat.

We were taught
it was where our mind sat

Amongst art deco buildings with a view
this was the neighborhood where I grew.

Between two currents,
the East river and the Hudson,
my thoughts flowed like a stream into an ocean

Entrepreneurs, I was influenced by.
Drug dealers kept the streets clean
            of robbers, rapists & thugs
Cops made deals to catch kingpins

And I? And I.
I became a little hustler.

My product? My imagination.

I grew to become a distributor of dreams
because I hung out with the fathers
at the number hole,
where the library and church
all resided on the same block
so you could learn math
read
and then pray
that your numbers hit

Bettina "Gold" Wilkerson

This is where I grew up
My experience, my life
En un lugar pequeno que se llama
Washington Heights

an AWAKENING

Today is Brand New & It's Yours

Breaking down walls
Bold
Working through fears
Cherishing true friendships
Being grateful for each day
Ready to give a hug
Ready to share some love
Crying when necessary
Laughing in the rain
Celebrating something good about you
Celebrating something good about me
Discovering what free is
Learning what we is
Dreaming because I can
Vast like the ocean
Ubiquitous like the universe
Flying above the clouds
Setting with the sun
Seeing You in Me
Seeing I in You
Being one
Undefined
Out of the box
Religious...less
Soulful
Spiritual
Determined
Born with vision
Capable of kicking our *own* ass
Thank you very much

Ready to listen
I have dreams
I know You do too

Pick one
Build on it
Start your own company
Do not be afraid of NO
say Yes Yes Yes
Persevere
Don't give up

We are not policies and procedures
We are human beings

Got an inside lock?
Here's the key
Unlock the door
Walk outside
Run outside
Take it all in
Deep breath—
Exhale
Inhale
Exhale
Look around
This is your space too
Design it the way You want
What do You see
See You
Feel You
Be You

Who's with me?
Let's go
Start now
Today is Brand New & It's Yours!

I M U ME LIFE

I riSE
giving thanks
I get to see another day
I riSE
blessed with new a thought
to do things a different way
Got a spring
flowing through my veins
let me be the faucet
u turn on
when u wish
to drink
the water from the rain

Refreshing
Invigorating
I M REVIVE
I M the uP
that will catch U on the way down
I m NOT caffeine
offering a temporary stimulation
I M organic
a natural occurrence
I did not just get here
I have been here
I M love
wading through the chaos

I M-I M-I M

I M that moment in time
standing at the precipice
when u have no choice
but to evolve

I M the thought
u thought
u never had
I M change
I M growth
I M the dash
between the beginning
and the end

I M the hot sun
and the cool moon
I M the stars
u don't see
during the day
but are still there
waiting for u
to reach up
and grab one
from the sky

I M movement
I M atmosphere
I M the ocean breeze
and the morning dew

I M brief
but elaborate
vulnerable with u
closed without u

I M desire
I M the hunger
I M the one
touching u in your dreams
I M the whisper in your ear
shouting to forward on

Bettina "Gold" Wilkerson

I M with U
as U are with ME
and together
WE
are
Life.

THE PASSAGE

We touch lives
while being touched by lives
during those moments
those connections
time stands still for no one

So what is the meaning of these connections
which become the thread woven into a patchwork
like the quilts our ancestors created
that told the stories of their lives

What is the meaning to—of—Life?

Life is perhaps a passage
an exploration affording us
the opportunity
to experience all of our senses
the taste, the touch, the smell
to see eachother
ourselves, the world
to listen, to differ
to embrace
to love, and be loved
maybe defines the meaning of our lives
and life itself, as well as, the direction it takes

So is the question "What is the meaning of life?"
or is it "What is my/our/your purpose in this life?
Are they one and the same?"

In the passage
we witness hope
in the seed that grows
from the crack of a concrete sidewalk
into a beautiful flower

Bettina "Gold" Wilkerson

In the passage
we can choose between solitary confinement,
deep fears that incarcerate our mind and spirit
and strip us of our freedom
OR
we can dream beyond the walls
that may have boxed us in
and build bridges instead
which will lead us on a different path

In the passage
courage is not found in acts of violence
but it is found in forgiveness

In the passage
we may not all be the same
but when we differ
it should be done
with a sense of dignity,
respect and kindness
the way the sun breaks through the clouds
and forms a rainbow
to complement the rain

In the passage
we are so blessed with the gift of breath
what we do with that breath
defines who we are

In the passage
death is not an end
it is simply an unknown
some say
it's going home

So those who have gone on
whose journey is complete

perhaps their leaving
is to remind us
to live a purposeful life
while we
are still
in this passage……

B U

I m complex
I m not flat nor one dimensional
I m beyond 4 corners
I change, I grow, I evolve
I have depth that even I can't see
I m consistently inconsistent
which enables me to stay the same
I m a stream of consciousness
with one common thread – ME

so B U

I aM Creation
(what life said to me one day in the shower)

I will never die on you
I will never go completely black
I will never cease to exist
I will resist

For I am the rock
you can build your foundation on
I am Lance Armstrong
I live long and strong
I am Duracell and Ever Ready
I am forever ready
and keep going on
and on
and on

I am the pulse, the beat, the flow
I am the thing in your heart that lets you know
I am that gut feeling
I am like water
fluid and streaming

I am the paint, the brush, the canvass
I am the ink, the pen, the scroll
I am the beginning of all time
and the end of nothingness

I am the tear that evolves into a resolve
I am your happiness undiscovered
I am the light
I am love
I am creation…

Undeniable

Incontestable
Irrefutable
like water is wet
hot is not cold
and the drum drives
the rhythm to the beat

I am the writing on the wall
the hieroglyphics
a pictorial of your history
indisputable
unquestionable
a descendent of the first people
my cousin is Lucy
not the one that made us laugh
and her cousin was Ardi
a little further back in her past
we are connected in our genome
returning us to one home
a common thread, a single root
from the same tree of life
where humanity began
where fear never stands

My words will never
feel like thorns or hands
pressed against barbed wire
I am the eye,
the window to the soul
reflection, enlightenment
an alternative to the fire

because gifts are abundant
we need to recognize

pause and take heed
find that peace inside

I know you want to be fast
like that star shooting across the sky
or the dream that never truly dies,
to be like Elvis and live residually…
but in the process find your truth
and live that
for it is our truth
that sets us free—
Undeniably.

I M A POET

Watching me from afar
I may appear to be crazy
as I stand on a corner
spitting my poetic prose
while waiting to cross the road
not within earshot
for you to pick up on

You try not to stare
but notice no one standing next to me...
No one appears to be there.
I catch you looking
and frankly Charlotte
and I said Charlotte not Scarlet
I don't give a damn.

I am a Poet.

I don't wish to converse with you
about my poetry
and discuss
rhythm, meters, similes
and metaphors
it will only serve
to let you know
I'm studied and intelligent

I prefer to spit
a collection of thoughts
sometimes random
other times specific

I find my words
in the quiet moments
in between the sounds

and the noise
that surrounds us all
the same way others
may find the sunlight
in between the raindrops

When I sleep
           I M a Poet
When I dream
           I M a Poet
When I awake
           I M a Poet
When I eat
           I M a Poet
and when I die
hopefully
I shall still be
a Poet.

I M a Poet who takes to heart
"the pen is mightier than the sword"
and the words we use
can either build up or tear down
and if we choose
to convey love
and/or disappointment
we should deliver our words
with the grace of a butterfly
landing on the petal of a flower

I M a Poet
who sits quietly in the corner
and purposefully go unnoticed
to scribe the essence of a room

the way a photographer
captures a moment in time

Bettina "Gold" Wilkerson

I M a Poet
who screams quietly
at the pain I claim not to feel
and in the same breath
confronts the fear
to facilitate a breakthrough
the way the ocean waves
create a new shoreline

I M a Poet
who looks for the footsteps
in the sand
to know
I m walking with God

So maybe I M
just a lil' crazy
or not
what I do know
though
is
I M A POET.

Truth & Pain

WHERE PAIN COMES FROM...

(lyrics)

When we fail to learn the lesson from the journey
Not to humble oneself to the truth
When anger burns deep in you like fire
But you won't grab hold to let go
and break through

Oh this is where your pain comes from

When you block the voice
shouting deep within you
stop listening to the whisper
you know you hear
when the eyes in the mirror
tell all your secrets
but you dress yourself
to see someone else standing there

This is where your pain comes from

Beauty is facing our challenges
Courage is working through our fears
Understand if you've been down
We've all had at least one up
So pain is so temporary my dear

I said...
Beauty is facing our challenges
Courage is working through the fears
Understand if we've been down
We've all had at least one up
So pain is so temporary my dear

When you feel there is a weakness in crying
So you shed no tears
and call it strong

judging others by your perfected illusion
taken back when the control loses
hold
hold
hold

This is where your pain comes from…

Broken...But Strong

You're Broken...but strong
trying to hold onto what you knew once
who you were once
defined by family
familiar walls
filled with pictures
of what you know now
as an illusion of joy
a false pretense
of a reality that never truly existed
You're Broken...but strong

Understanding that the past
no longer exist
you stand at a crossroad
wondering who you will become
and how will you get there
you pause to cry a tear

Do you embark upon the road less traveled
or do you stay on the road of familiarity
familiarity seems to offer a sense of safety
even when that which you are familiar with
no longer is good for you...
a familiar pain...a familiar betrayal...
a familiar fear of discovery...of newness

You choose the road less traveled
& forge ahead...alone
broken...but strong.

Don't Feel Bad for Me

I was born with a chronic illness
do not know how it got there
but it got there anyway
there is no cure
A seed of imperfections,
but perfection in God's eyes
So don't feel bad for me

I've had 13 surgeries in a span of 20 years;
I probably have more bolts and screws
from my waist down
than some of you
have in your toolbox in your homes
but don't feel bad for me

Feel bad for the one
who sees an opportunity
but is too afraid to seize it
due to fear of failure.
Feel bad for the person
who has so much noise in their head
we call R.U.F.U.S.
Robbing U from Ultimate Success
they choose to stand still
instead of moving forward
No don't feel bad for me

Feel bad for the worker
who's been downsized
upsized
squeezed wide

ismed
schismed
and snatched from their realism

Bettina "Gold" Wilkerson

Do not feel bad for me

Feel bad for the one
who is afraid to dream
because they are too busy
living in their nightmares
No don't feel bad for me

Feel bad for the child of a mother
who does not know how to be a mother
because her mother was a mother
who had a mother
who did not know how to be a mother,
or of a father
who is never there
But Please do not
feel bad for me

Feel bad for the woman or man
who is trapped in their own despair
anguish, anger, bitterness, sadness or fear
whose horizon looks more like a cliff
you fall off of
rather than something you can see beyond
like the Vikings, Spaniards, and Africans
who saw the world
and boldly went
where no man has gone before
Do not feel bad for me

Feel bad for the children of families
who have lived through foreclosures
whose stability has been uprooted
by insidious corporate greed
But Don't Feel Bad for Me

Feel bad for the souls
of SOME… of our congressmen, senators
and politicians
who have gotten so lost
in their own tunnel vision
they no longer see the light
at the end of the tunnel
Do not feel bad for me

Feel bad for the people
who have become reactionary
and manipulated by the idea
that the "MEXICAN"
is the reason we do not have jobs

Who will be our next group?
Don't…Feel Bad…for me

Feel bad for the persons
who are unemployed
by no doing of their own
and who are now
being described as
shiftless, lazy…
and on drugs?

Welcome to our new classism.

I've had 13 surgeries in a span of 20 years;
I probably have more bolts and screws
from my waist down
than some of you have in the toolbox
in your homes

But I've been blessed

Bettina "Gold" Wilkerson

I see
and understand things
others don't get
or don't want to get
I have a vision
I have dreams
I LIVE...

So Don't
Feel Bad for Me.

Off the Pain

Push the button
Morphine
push the button
Morphine
creating more fiends
I take straight codeine
got the opposite of
an auto immune deficiency disease
got an hyper immune
it seems
so it consumes me
by any means
like a parasite
eating its own skin to breathe

But I survive

pharmaceutical pushers
peddling their new technology
under the guise of an organic biology
calling me on my cell
to sell me their ideology
like a street pharmacist
on the corner
distributing his toxicology

who's more insidious
I don't know
you tell me
but thank god I regained
and now I'm
off the pain.

Loneliness...

In a room filled with a thousand people,
I heard her whisper
"I feel....
.......alone......."

What is Fear?

does it linger in the darkness of our thoughts
like a burglar waiting to rob us of our most
precious gifts

is it the abyss, the unknown, a journey yet to be
discovered, a path never walked upon

does its mere presence teach how to overcome
and become fearless

What is fear?

does it create cobwebs out of visions once
thought of as beautiful and innovative

as we look deep into the eyes-the window to the
soul, is it the love we no longer see in ourselves

is it not knowing what you don't know, therefore,
you don't know what you need to know

What is fear?

is it living life with a dream
unfulfilled...unrequited love,
the lack of human touch upon the flesh

is it an eagle discovering it has a broken wing
or a squirrel that simply cannot find enough nuts
to store for the winter

What is fear?

does it manifest in expressions of hate,
indifference and intolerance

Bettina "Gold" Wilkerson

does it melt slowly away our spirit like the heat
emanating from the wick's fire on a candle
liquefying the wax-dripping until there is nothing
left

Fear
what is it?

I believe it's everything, all things
we allow our mind to make it out to be...

Love is so many things

At Dawn

I gaze at your picture
as if looking beyond the horizon
waiting for the sun at dawn.
knowing I will feel the warmth
of something so beautiful,
but yet...
not within arm's reach,
I patiently wait.

The hues in your hair
reflect the colors of the sky;
your eyes become the ocean-
I dive in and swim in the direction of your soul...
it is there I shall search for the key to your heart.
I bury myself in you like a grain of sand
in an oyster's shell
so when you open,
I will be that precious pearl
you see and desire,
to keep with you forever.

There in your soul
I shall scribe love sonnets
that will become lullabies in your subconscious
to help you rest peacefully at night
and you will awake in the morning
in harmony with your spirit
hearing melodies throughout your day.

When I find the key to unlock your door,
you will feel me touching you
the way fire warms a cool breeze;
but not like a raging blaze
which is all too consuming-
I am much too subtle for that...

the crackling of my embers
will be there to remind you to keep me burning.

So for now…I resign
to holding the image of your face
surrendering to this moment
like sitting on the beach
looking beyond the ocean
waiting for the sun
to creep up on the horizon…
at dawn.

WORTHY

WE
are all in the making
being processed, packaged
shot down a conveyor belt
to the assembly line
where we shall be
squeezed, poked, prodded,
pulled, dropped, slammed,
and tested for durability.

Occasionally,
our hearts
will make guest appearances
throughout the lines of love poems and sonnets...
and maybe, if I could be so lucky,
my heart would be delivered to you.

I would arrive at your doorstep
and you would receive me
take me in and unwrap me;
I could curl up next to you
and be the blanket that keeps you warm.

Maybe I could be that soft place
you choose to rest your head upon-
like a cloud...a pillow
maybe I could be like fresh water
in the morning caressing your skin
maybe I could be the dream
you never want to awake from
or I could be the wine
that relaxes you after a long day.

Maybe I could be the scent
you identify as home

the food you need to sustain you—
eat me, drink me
bathe in my river
let me wash away your fear
maybe in fifty years
I could be
that rocking chair.

Maybe I could be for you
what you are for me
a reflection
a reminder
that we are all
worthy of love.

Connections

                    at
            the
            Core
        you
    oscillate in me
            you
    never misunderstanding
    the need
    to exhibit clearly
    expressions of emotion
    touching my soul intuitively
    with   a   sensitivity   that
    overlays
    every nuance
    lying between us
            I
    vacillate between
    the reality of what you want
            and
    my reality of where I am
    yet still
            you
    grow in me
    like a synapse
    fusing our connections

THEY STOOD

They stood
quietly and erect
motionless and emotionless
bearing the loneliness during the winter storms
learning to appreciate the bitter cold
discovering…a beauty in it,
they stood.

On windy days, they stood
on rainy days, they stood
on beautiful springs days
amongst the lilies in the field, they stood
On sweltering summer days, they stood
as the leaves transitioned to fall, they stood.
Loyal to a fault
dedicated to the servitude of one master
they stood.

Until one day…
a woman came along
stopped in front of them
and said
"You've been standing there for many days;
weariness is showing in the lines on your face.
Tomorrow I shall bring stools so you may rest."
Then she turned and walked away.

The news of the woman with the stools
began to spread throughout,
a panic ensued—

There cannot be any breaking of the rules
I promptly showed up
to display my disposition

demanding that they still stand
in spite of their condition.

The next day came
you could feel the stir
and the unrest
the woman
with the stools
made a promise
that she kept-
Having grown fatigued from standing
they descend and relent
into a deep slumber
they quickly went.

In that instance...I felt
a presence within
desperately I tried to awake them
I shook and shook to no end...
With no protection around
no place to run
I fell in love
when my guards relinquished their guns—
I fell in love
when they...
no longer stood.

Haikus

At dawn, touch the soil
It's the beginning of time
embrace the newness

Hearts beat together
with a rhythmic pulse of love
I scream out her name

Crisp clean organic
like spring water with a bite
perfection....sake

Pool, geometry
Isosceles triangle
call corner pocket

My feet hurt, legs hurt
tired of walking, walk on
your job is not done

35 Years
(for Tree and Sharon Arrington)

If marriage was built like the pyramids, it would
be perfect
It would be carefully calculated the way Imhotep,
the great Egyptian architect,
configured the Step Pyramids—
creating a foundation to withstand the test of
time.

Your marriage, your union
has been built upon moments strung together like
pearls—
seconds that have evolved into 352,800 minutes
5,880 hours
1,820 weeks
12,740 days…
35 years

But marriage is more like the Nile
a resource for life
flowing and discovering new terrain
finding its ebb and flow
spawning streams the way a tree grows branches
it is fluid at its best
turbulent at its most challenging times
but it always reaches the same point where it
empties
to become something larger than itself -
love
home

It may not always be as perfect as
Thelonious Monk's "Round Midnight"
or
Ella Fitzgerald's impeccable phrasing and
intonation…

Marriage may not always move with the grace of
a dancer
like Katherine Dunham or Alvin Ailey

But your union, your legacy
through better or worse
thick or thin
hot or cold
stands in tribute of our elders
who may have jumped the broom

35 years
12,740 days
1,820 weeks
5,880 hours
352,800 minutes
all built upon seconds.

What it says to me
is...
I got your back.

Those lil' Things
(lyrics)

I love the way you run your fingers through my
hair;
the look in your eyes that says you care
the way you whisper, the way you smile
I love your quiet times and when you break wild-
the way you curl up next to me when you sleep
the intellectual look when you read
the way you laugh, the way you cry
the way your mouth moves when you speak
what's on your mind—

Love...
is about those lil' things.

Thoughts about LOVE

Throughout history
it's seem like a mystery
when we move against universal love
it's like committing blasphemy
Now I know you can understand me
but I want you to feel me
because I know if you feel me
you'll understand me
Do you feel me?
may I speak with you about love

From that very first breath
life appears to be one long test
we study the things we don't know
learn from our mistakes so we may grow
like Jack and Jill tumbling down the hill
we always clean up after the spill
through heartache and pain,
fear and disdain
it's our quest for love
that keeps us in this game
it's our quest for love
that keeps us in this game
may I speak with you about love

I believe in the teachings of Jesus Christ
but I'm not a big fan of religion
No, don't hate
some of the most deadliest wars
have been fought for religion
some say religion is a contradiction
to everything love is

how many wars
who's keeping score

killing in the name of the Lord
we fear the anti-Christ
but sometimes it is that fear
which makes our behavior anti-Christ
judging those who are different from you
everyday
trying to slay the souls of those who don't see
things your way

We can hope for a better tomorrow
or start living a better today
plant and water the seeds
to nurture our dreams
try to figure out what this living thing means
Life is an exploration of the mind
that is where the heart truly lies
because it doesn't take much
to show a little kindness
it takes so much more
to be a little mindless
how we evolve is up to me and you
those decisions aren't made in a voting booth
may I speak with you about love

Last but not least
let me leave with this peace
be for you unselfishly first
never to make yourself last
for if we cannot take care of ourselves
the odds are we cannot take care of anyone else

and if you give a gift based upon your needs
you never gave a gift at all

I hope to be a faucet of inspirational knowledge
I did not learn this in college
sometimes love renders us speechless

a moment of pause…
standing still in a state of awe
like a ray of sun bursting from within
love is the synapse
it is the connection
it's the one being one with one
standing outside yourself
to see yourself, to free yourself
to find within yourself
that the beginning of all you
is love.

I wish to thank you for allowing me
to share my thoughts with you about
Love.

entitled "Friend"

You were like a poem in my heart
the one I knew I would never have to scribe
because it would always be there-
entitled "Friend"

You would be the word I would never forget
I would never have to snap my fingers
to recall you—

You reminded me of stained glass
colorful—permanent
etched to stand the test of time

Your journey is written with an indelible ink
a life that will never be washed away
I still dance to your favorite tunes
and laugh at the recollection of the sound of your
voice saying—"You so silly"
and even though I still hear you,
I often wonder where you went…

You are like a poem in my heart
the one I knew I would never have to scribe
because it would always be there—
entitled "Friend."

The Hug

we may not all be alike;
it is okay that we differ;
we can be respectful;
we can be understanding;
we share the same planet;
we share the same oxygen;
we are human beings-
this connection is our common thread,
the hug.

For Those
Who Blazed the Path
For Me To Walk Upon

The Image of My Mother

I wish to share with you
an image of my mother.

for 23,760,000 seconds,
I laid in her womb
evolving…
waiting for the dawn of light

when I opened my eyes
I saw her smile
I learned to play Mozart
by studying her ivories

her arms stretched
are like the bow of violin
to me she is music

petite in stature
but she is grand like the piano
her steps
taught me how to take great strides

her eyes are like the universe
pupils, the galaxies
in them I see the stars
on the darkest of nights

steady like a ship sailing on the ocean blue
she is the vessel that brought me ashore

my life is documented
in the lines of her face
they are the hieroglyphics of our family—
our history, her story

as a child, my favorite place to rest my head
was upon the scars beneath her navel
for that is where she bore my sister's life
that spot became my pillow
a soft place for me to dream
she is my brother's keeper
a village that raised a child

she reminds me of the Baobab tree
roots planted firmly in the rich soil
I often climb her branches
to get a different view of the world
her laughter is sweet like her cocoa skin
I taste her love with every breath
she is the artist who sculpted my mind
like Rodin sculpting "The Thinker"

her words
are like warm tea on a frigid day

she is my best friend
and I love her
close your eyes
do you see her now
that
is the image of my mother...

The Drum Beats a Rhythm, I Can

The drum beats a rhythm
    that tells my heart

          I Can

the drum beats a rhythm
    that tells my heart

          I Can

the drum beats a rhythm
    that tells my heart

          I Can!

I
  Can
I
  Can
I
  Can
I
  Can

The drum beats a rhythm
that tells my heart I can.

I can be like Harriet Tubman running
But I'm not running—
I am creating, not escaping.
She gave me that option years ago
with her sacrifice
so I may grow up
and walk on water like Christ
because he was so D.O.P.E. and nice
Displaying
Outstanding
Possibilities
Everywhere

Tapped me on the shoulders
pointed me to the stars

And said there are the stairs.
With faith the size of a mustard seed
you can move mountains
build igloos on deserts
turn raindrops into beads of gold
and create the greatest stories
that will ever be told.

I am a descendent of the keenest mathematicians;
did you not know that?
Recognize.

They figured the equations
build pyramids from a grain of sand
set atop a transmitter
to send me messages
through the rhythm of the beat of the drum
telling my heart I Can.

The drum beats a rhythm
      that tells my heart

           I Can

the drum beats a rhythm
      that tells my heart

           I Can

the drum beats a rhythm
      that tells my heart

           I Can!

I
  Can
I
  Can
I
  Can
I
  Can

Bettina "Gold" Wilkerson

The drum beats a rhythm
that tells my heart

I can.

Claudette Colvin

She thought it was a birth right
freedom
with feet that were feeling so tired
baby in the bun
never thought she was the one
to take a stand
against the white man
to take a stand
for what was right then
damn
she was the first
and her name
is Claudette Colvin

Our history is permanent
like stained glass
that will never change
etched with memories
of injustice & victories
healed wounds &
scars left from a time past
but still present
in the shackles
closed steel doors
which have become
institutionalized
concentration camps
filled with the emaciated minds
of young Black American youth
who are still seeking their emancipation
not realizing that its comes through
their education

the knowing of someone like U
the knowing of someone like U
the knowing of someone like U

Claudette Colvin
who stood and stood
who stood and stood
then sat
so we
could get up
and walk
heads up
no longer shuffle
yes sir
no ma'am
open doors
walk through
closed doors
whites only
blacks here
Browder vs Gayle
1956—Supreme Court
thank God
we have overcome
still grow
America knows
when things ain't right
right

America knows
when things ain't right
right

homicide
legal assassinations

Amadou Diallo
Michael Stewart

Michael Griffith
Travon Martin
whose blood flow
into the drains
like rain after a storm
washing away
tragedies
that once occurred here
which now become faint memories
except for the loved ones
where loss becomes deep pain
creating a crack in the heart
like a crevice in the arctic ice
the resting place of a cold chill

but we shall not forget U
because…

Our history is permanent
like stained glass
that will never change
etched with memories
of injustice & victories
healed wounds and
scars left from a time past
but still present

and you are still present…

Claudette Colvin
who stood & stood
who stood & stood
then sat

Bettina "Gold" Wilkerson

so we
may elevate
walk
and forward on...

MY LOCS SOUND NICE

My locs sound nice

                check 1

My locs sound nice

                check 2

She wears her locs like a lion's mane
Shoulders back, head lifted
pointed straight forward
An evolution is always taking place in her stride
They swing like a pendulum
so her thoughts are free flowing

On occasion in elevators of corporate buildings
her cerebral state of mind
is randomly interrupted by

Excuse me
I love your hair
how do you get it like that—

May I touch…

No
but thank you
but No—

You cannot touch my hair.

You see…
these strands are sacred stories
like this one here—
whose roots extend back to 1619
when the first documented slave ship
landed on the shores of North America in
        Jamestown, Virginia

Bettina "Gold" Wilkerson

I hear Kings and Queens
who became cotton pickers
singing Negro spirituals
under the hot sun while beads of sweat
formed on their foreheads
and glistened like diamonds
to remind them of their royalty…
Majestic

And this one—
this one reps the lexicon of my people
with sayings like
Gotta catch the kitchen in the back,
kinky roots and naps,
Oh you got snaps!
The Juba Dance and jive talk…
We are vibrant and brilliant
and our hair is as diverse
as the hues of our skin
from blue black to high yellow
and everything in between
All natural
All beautiful
We are the braids
and cornrows plaited together
We stay connected
throughout the ghettos of the world

And this one—
this one is the Scholar
sharing knowledge like water
streaming from a faucet
letting us know that Blacks
were not the first to reside in the ghetto.

We were preceded by the Jews,
the Italians, the Asians, and the Irish

So we don't have to stay here
if we don't choose to…
The GHETTO is a mentality.

And this one—
Malcolm, Martin
reminding me of the sacrifice they made
to stand tall like a California Redwood tree
strong, capable, able, conscious to understand
that an injustice to one is an injustice to all

Sojourner Truth, Harriet Tubman,
Madam C.J. Walker, Nikki Giovanni,
Sonia Sanchez, Debra Lee, Oprah Winfrey,
Cicely Tyson, Whitney Houston,
Angela Davis, Queen Latifah
Shirley Chisholm—
the first Black female congress woman,
Shirley Chisholm

Trailblazers!
Trailblazers!

Oh wait a minute…
I have one more
This little one…this little one right here.

This is the future.
Today's urban youth, this is hip-hop
this is jazz, music, the spoken word
the poet, the griot
the student, the teacher, the doctor
the lawyer, the CEO
the nonprofit worker, the community worker
the volunteer, the entrepreneur
the nurse, the athlete
the blue collar worker, the minister

the homosexual, the heterosexual, the lesbian
the transgender, the bisexual
the mulatto, el Moreno
the disabled, the homeless, the caregivers
the caregivers who envelope our spirit in a warm
      blanket
and rock it like a baby in a cradle while singing
      sweet lullabies
and sharing their stories in order to teach us how
to create our own stories
THIS is my community.

So no,
You cannot touch my hair.

You see, my kinky roots are like a microphone
converting the voices in my head into an energy
which is then amplified allowing my ancestors
      stories to stay present
that's why I keep my locs hanging over my ears
so they will always know that
I AM Listening!

My locs sound nice

               check 1

My locs sound nice

               check 2

Yeah.

Where do WE go from Here?

Walk

    with me

        in peace...

I have found my place in life
and that is, to be here...
with you.

When My Soul Speaks, I Scribe...*Poetry*

When my soul speaks,
I have no choice but to be the vessel that breathes
her life
my mind descends into a deep trance while being
fully awake
only to watch as my hand glides across the page
allowing the ink to form words which constructs
the story she chooses to tell.

When my soul speaks,
she commands I surrender to the pen and
relinquish all rights to this existence
supplies all the oxygen I need
keeps my blood pure with the touch of every pen
stroke
that becomes a quiet drumbeat maintaining the
perfect rhythm for my heart
I surrender to her demands.

When my soul speaks,
a metamorphosis takes place
butterflies are set free
I hear colors like red, blue, yellow, purple,
orange, black
they become the sound of her voice
the inflection in her tone
a melody if she chooses to sing...

I find myself surrounded by a cacophony
in a social setting that suddenly becomes silent
when she enters the room
heads turn; you can hear a pin drop
Someone whispers "who's that?"
"Oh that...that is my soul;
She is the ivories that perfect note

Bettina "Gold" Wilkerson

like Ella's scat, she spits fiyah
there's no water that can douse out her flames
she is indigo, the auroras,
warm like a ray of sun
her light surrounds the earth in a halo
Davinci's 'Mona Lisa'
Ellington's 'A Train'
soft as a baby's bottom
giving with a heart of gold
she is pure
she is pure
and this soul...oh this soul
when she is done,
I shall be done
this, I know
so when my soul speaks,
I scribe...poetry"

FRUIT
(who do we become)

Most are taught we eat fruit
not that we can be fruit
we can be like the grape
growing together in clusters
all interconnected
a community

We can be like the orange-
vibrant- rich with nourishment
to live a healthy life
a thirst quencher

We can be the fresh apple
whose seeds will plant food for thought
and grow young trees
with branches
that will grow more apples

We can be the kiwi, the raspberry,
the grapefruit, the sweet peach,
the cherry, the nectarine, the plum,
the blackberry, the pineapple, the tangerine

We can be like any fruit we choose to be
therefore, I leave you with this…
don't simply eat fruit
go out into the world and be fruit

May each one of us
possess the assets- the qualities
to teach one of us
may we embrace the gift of life
the opportunities
to learn something new every day

Bettina "Gold" Wilkerson

For it is the student
who teaches the teacher how to teach
therefore, learn, grow, and flourish
enrich the society and our community
with the nutrients
from the heart and mind

YOU ARE FRUIT!
I AM FRUIT!
WE ARE FRUIT!
RECOGNIZE
and ALWAYS REPRESENT!!!

26 Mics N 26 Weeks
(my reality)

I was born with a horn in my hand
knew I would be a star
knew I would journey far
many dues were paid
on this road I paved
I see patterns in my brain
hear rhythmic sounds
that form words onto my tongue
flowing out like a river
to quench the thirst of the souls
who live for the word
who lives for the poet
who lives for the poet
who lives for the word

I never stopped believing
into winning
I close my eyes
and it's the world I am seeing
grew up in the hood
prep school educated
fell in love, raised two kids
then we got separated
full circle, I'm back on stage
behind the mic
I'm living a different phase
using my voice is my only choice
another dream so it seems
I'm on 26 Mics N 26 Weeks

Been scribing since the age of ten
I draft stories from the beginning to the end
connecting phrases like streams to rivers
taking minds on a journey

Bettina "Gold" Wilkerson

like "Moby Dick's" Melville
they say "it only takes a dollar and a dream"
well I'm not banking on the dollars
I'm banking on the seeds
I'm a farmer
who's planted them throughout the years
rising before each dawn to sow my fields
and now I'm on a journey
to watch what I sowed yield
because like Maya
I understand why a caged bird sings
peering through the bars
hoping her poelodies form wings
and finds a perch for her dreams

Get lifted and fly away with me
cuz I'm on 26 Mics N 26 Weeks

I won't stop
til my days have come to rest
and my words will be left
to form bridges and paths
for dreamers to walk upon
like Dorothy and Toto
on the yellow brick road
where there is hope
there is a way
where there is will
there is determination

we are the people
of one great global nation
planet earth is where we live
one world
one vibe
one love

one poem at a time
across this great expanse
and my words will dance
to the music emanating from your souls
tapping into your greatness is what sets me free

that's why
I'm on 26 Mics N 26 Weeks!
;-)

GLOSSARY

Poelody: a spoken word poem (free verse) that contains lyrical/melodic phrasing which can be accompanied by music

Artivist: artist activist, who uses their art not only to entertain, but also to inspire, uplift, motivate, educate and engage a community in heartfelt dialogue and action regarding issues which impact the quality of their lives, as well as, to initiate/facilitate change that is conducive for a productive and harmonious society.

ABOUT THE AUTHOR

Bettina Wilkerson, also known as Poet Gold or Gold, is a published writer, spoken word performance artist, poet, and community "artivist". She is an active member of the Dutchess County Arts Council and the Artist Action Group. Her work is driven by the desire to triumph over personal challenges and her belief that everyone has greatness inside of them. Through Gold's performance and writing, she grabs you by the heart and says "Recognize."

Facebook: Bettina Gold Wilkerson
You Tube: bgoldw's channel
Email: bgoldwpoetry@gmail.com

ACKNOWLEDGMENTS

Neil "Sleuth Pro" Johnson whose creative and poetic platform empowered me to acknowledge I still had wings to fly. Michael White, an incredible artist, who created the front and back cover of this book. Elton Igunbor, an amazing photographer who captures my every move. Cate Fricke, my editor, who helped with the presentation of this book.

My family,Wilkerson and Ware—I love you more. The "Mighty Team"—Joyce Wilkerson, Doreene Thompson, Henry Wilkerson, Martrice, Rosana Almonte, Marlen Bodden, Stacey Cummings, Vera, Machi Tantillo, Terri Joyner, Michael and Joyce Stern, Nikita Miles, Gwen Santana, Sonya and Dee, Darshan Russell, Leon Lee Sills, Michael and Kiriaki Pertesis, Luvleeh Poetiklocks, Rock Wilk, Bob Auchincloss, Caleb Holcombe, Stephanie Myricks, Katharine McCarthy, Debora Flores, Myra Adams, Charles Bannerman, Caroline "Red" Rice, Valerie Melendez, Angela Melendez— without all of you this first book m ay not have happened.

Starz Beyond Nation and Joanne Grell for believing in the dream. Aissa Huerta, for sitting with me while I wrote late nights and being my sounding board; Shawn Cullen (Amici's Pizzeria); my medical team—Dr. Brandt, Dr. Munne and Dr. Hassan-thank you for following your call to heal; for your leadership and support—the Dutchess County Arts and Community Action Group (We are Artivists), Linda and Scott Marston-Reid, and the Dutchess County Arts Council. Last, but certainly not least, my business manager—Robert Montgomery, we are meant to be on this journey together.

29042840R10065

Made in the USA
Middletown, DE
05 February 2016